Dedicated to Napoleon

Flowers Aren't Always Beautiful

Elliott Paulson

Flowers Aren't Always Beautiful
Published by Elliott Paulson.

Copyright ©2024 Elliott Paulson. All rights reserved.

This is a work of fiction. Names, characters, businesses, places, events, locales, and incidents are either the products of the author's imagination or used in a fictitious manner. Any resemblance to actual persons, living or dead, or actual events is purely coincidental.

No part of this book may be reproduced in any form or by any mechanical means, including information storage and retrieval systems without permission in writing from the publisher/author, except by a reviewer who may quote passages in a review.

All images, logos, quotes, and trademarks included in this book are subject to use according to trademark and copyright laws of the United States of America.

ISBN: 979-8-218-34756-7

Cover and interior design by Victoria Wolf, wolfdesignandmarketing.com, copyright owned by Elliot Paulson.

> All rights reserved by Elliott Paulson.
> Printed in the United States of America.

This collection of poems
was written while I was in a severe depression.

Today, December 3rd, 2023,
I am on the other side of it.

Proceeds from the sales of this collection will go to
The American Foundation for Suicide Prevention

"Write hard and clear about what hurts."
—Ernest Hemingway

EYES OF THE GLASS MOON

i think about loneliness
and all the people
who i will never meet
since i've been so timid
       and insecure.
i hope there is unification in death.

no one looks anyone in their eyes anymore.
       my eyes are suns.
       your eyes are suns.

as i caress myself
i relieve the loneliness of this leg,
       pop an ingrown hair
to prepare my body
for the time someone will touch me here;

       i stare
into the night sky.
there is a moon.

and here i am, at home
in front of this curtainless window
naked and alone

revealing to this city
the side of myself
society is forbidden to see.

reflections always remind me
of every mistake i've come to make.

and i remember it has been seventeen days
since i have touched the skin of another,
       felt the warmth of a stranger –

in this windowpane
       are my
       translucent eyes.

ANGELIC ABORTION

amongst my family
i feel i am nothing near to a member.
my father and i have only played together
when it is time to shovel the driveway-snow;
so, i moved away to where there is no winter.

as my brother and i are children
in the back of our backyard
on our swing set,
long leg spiders infest it.
he pulls their legs off one by one,
      and dangles their still twitching single legs
      in between my eyes
      just to remind me that he is older;

into the forest i ran away with my golden plastic sword.
to where the bears sleep with each other
where the poison ivy grows so innocent
and the raspberries are black and waiting for me always;

i sit atop the highway's end
as i wait for transportation   from anyone,
anyone who has a warm hand,
who knows nothing of me.
my happiness isn't found in any hands here.

a nightmare i have tells me of how to be free of my fears,
a yellow-orb glows in the corner of my blackened bedroom,
there i stand in terror listening.
every angel is absent.

i am no longer afraid.
a long, long time ago,
i let my inner child die, so,
i could survive.

SONG OF BLOOD

in bed i lay now,
i pop another pimple on my cheek,
with blood upon my left thumb,
while i think about
what it means
to be a father;

i think of my past lovers while i am in rooms alone.
girls who have scars of a once slit wrist,
who has hatred in their eyes that can be seen even in darkness;
my heart of delusion believes it can cure everyone.

come.
i'll wear your trauma.　　　　　i'll wear your bruises.
　　　i'll wear everything
　　　you don't want to remember.

we will wear matching tennis shoes.
we will hold hands.
　　　our uniformed steps
　　　will inform this city
　　　we are two people
　　　who see beauty
　　　in the presence of scars,
because you are next to me
a laugh will be in my heart

that only a healing heart can have.

nestle up against   this pale tattooed flesh of mine
and with your entire body
embrace me as your newfound place of rest.

from our union
people will question
their faith in religion,

while we will question
         a future family.

you kiss my neck,
and again,
i kiss your forehead.
we lay flush naked,
your back against my stomach,
and both of us know
we need never to be ashamed
of where we bled from.

i caress your inner thighs
and run my fingers
along your scars

as if they are
strings of a harp.

CONVERSATIONS WITH SATAN

i am wearing great grandmother's clothing.
i am the year 1937,
you're amused by my imitation   though

i never received your invitation
to be loved unconditionally by you.

i know i am nothing more   than your
convenient   free
sideshow attraction
though still i dance.

i lie to you   and you
and him and her
as i pretend to enjoy this life.

i plead to hear strangers lust after me,
          every innocent cell in my body
          has been murdered
          by bright red
          pornography.

my love, once we are together,
i will sacrifice our first child
once he or she is born

for you will be the only one
who has never left me,
        don't be afraid of my departure
        i will lie and tell you
        the love i have for you
        isn't dependent   on your physical presence.

i am too afraid of judgement
to be vulnerable with anyone,
so,
ask me your existential questions
so,
        i may tell you "the right answers"
        so, you may believe i am a man
        who is more powerful than he really is.

my loneliness forces me to sit here quiet in silence,
alone with these demons in my thoughts.

i am a gardener
        in a war,
i am a human
        in a hell.

        tell me
how to silence these flames
        and i
        will obey your name.

RED RAINBOW

friday night
i am
on this iron fire escape
with these two fingers
and their scent   of burnt cigarettes;

i wear the black velour sweatpants now,
those that you wore
while you were asleep topless
      atop my unframed mattress;

you gave a comfort to me.
it let me believe you meant it
went you said
"i want to stay here.",
      but now
           i don't know where you are.

i cure myself
with self-abuse;

i *cut* across the top of my left foot
with the blade from a face-razor
while seated in this bathtub,

an all-red rainbow
of
a hundred shades
       runs wet.

this body bleeds.
       release envelops me.
       i become god.

       freedom
       from this skin prison,
       i become an innocent child again.

my self-love
       has a viscosity
       of blood.

CREMATE ME NOW

in church i kiss her
and i am too young to know
this is how my path of sin begins;

we ran away   from what was being preached,
into the church's empty nursery room,
she and i will die   without speaking of what happened.

how beautiful that sunday afternoon was.
while you sat on my lap
as i began to caress your tongue with mine.
how beautiful the breaking of our innocence was.

but now i'm left to live unsafe in this body,
as i walk with this crucifix of guilt
splintering into my bare back.

i have sacrificed my devotion to religion
so, i could receive separation from
the feeling of being in this blasphemous skin;

and i am thankful for this new morning
as it is another opportunity
for me to dream
the dream
of *my own assassination;*

god, finally show me

i am too much of a danger to you.

BLISTERED EYES

in london i am a boy,
a 14-year-old boy
on vacation
in a dressing room.
i pop a yellow pimple upon the mirror
and see myself
so hideous *here*.

my aunt and i take a tour of an underground dungeon,
    "here the slaves were covered in sores
    and blisters, looked just like
    him." the tour guide said
    as she points to me –

i still have the acne scars on my cheeks from when i wasn't beautiful.
i still have the scars on my heart from all the times strangers stared.

remember, i covered my face with my hands and explained
nothing is wrong. no, nothing is wrong. everything is fine.
all while you didn't know
thoughts of a healing-suicide
grew in my mind.

i learned what expectations are
far too soon into childhood,
i felt sorrow for who i saw in the mirror
long before i ever saw him with a blemish,

there is too much blood in my memories.
i pushed everyone away so i wouldn't have to bleed on them.

i want to be loved. an ornate love, full of touch.

i kept eye contact as we had sex, so you knew i cared for you.
                        beauty is made from vulnerability.
when you left
you said, "i'll see you soon", but
it's been nineteen months since then
     and still
     those words of yours
     have not come true.

STOLEN VIRGIN

do you remember when we were 13
on opposing sides of the couch
watching pornography together?

i don't know what is happening to my body.
and your parents are upstairs asleep.

    we are growing up too fast.

at 29 now,   i masturbate violent
and become suicidal again.

i need a bathtub for a baptism,
nonjudgmental weight of water
force my head down below survival,
    warm water cleanses me.
    o', the amount i love you,
    you may never know.
    —

there is a stone in my throat,
at the bottom-right corner
just below my adam's apple.   a secret sin.

i was just a child back then,
and now, i am an unrecognizable man.

and now,
here i am,
misdirected
because of what i believed
heaven was;

please, grab my hand,
        grab any part of me,

pull me away,
to anywhere
true kindness is.

DEATH DOVE

lungs expand as i stand
consume cigarette fumes
carbon monoxide poison
bloom of self-abuse again

against my left temple
a strike of a sledgehammer
while worms convulse within me
and this left hip
has a rusted dull knife
twisted into it

i reminisce over childish dreams
that died from suicidal depression

i pray
i become the death dove
black in flight

outside this window
i hear you, ambulance
      your call
      your tune

no mother
will ever dance to
and still
      you play on
      for someone

siren fades off
into the far end of the street

this city is given a remembrance
of fragility

red and blue lights
symbolize *"everything is fine."*
while someone is dying
on the inside.

EXPIRED TOUCH

my stomach is   it is
       as if it is
       filled
with other people's hair.
hair stuffed to the top
of this neglected esophagus,
i feel another compulsion to twitch –

i sit on my bed
thinking of who
i could have been
       when someone once held my hand,
had touched my finger.
in my younger   innocent years
i once was a dancer too,
       before i grew concerned
       of opinions people have –
       demons i believed i could hear.

hear those engines rev now
outside this open window.

those people in a rush
to reach those places
        where we,
where we will never meet each other.

i swallow prescription medications
far too inconsistent,
        i prevent their cure from occurring.

on my calendar
in permanent black marker
i have written:
        kill yourself on august 32nd.

i hope no one remembers me,
        i hope for so many
        great things.

DIVINE IMPRISONMENT

as a boy i jump on our parent's bed
wearing every one of our mother's brassieres.
you blackmail me with photography
in my older years.

every other day
i'll take a fifty-dollar-bill
out of your wooden briefcase in your room,
you are the richest teenager i know
until
there is no money of yours
left for me to steal.

my brother and i
have taught each other
family is a meaningless bond.

i run
run on the sidewalk
and the streets
and through parks
and darkness,

when my bones are ready for rest
i will set fire to this body
and let this tired spirit free.

it is 2:10 a.m.
and i am here
alone with this voice in my head
which whispers insistent
"you are stupid
and worthless!"..

while i am twelve and fifteen and seventeen years old
i sleep on my bedroom's floor every night,

at twenty i awake
out from another overdose
and i am seated at the wheel
of mother's red convertible.

(god's intension is to keep me alive
for a reason   i've yet to realize.)

> god,   *you still are my worst enemy.*

GOD OF GOLD

in my apartment's bathroom
as i dye my blond hair lavender

i see someone new in the mirror
who has the same scars on his cheeks as i do
and the same gaze in his aged eyes,
      i kiss the lips of the man in the glass.

i have tried to beautify my face
with ornate black ink distractions,

god must wonder:
      what happened to my creation?

i remember the photo of me as a child,
3 years old without self-abuse
in a blue pin-stripe-suit,
i am sorry and so sorry to that boy
who is no longer divine.

now,
i disguise my outsides
with emblems of what you believe
represents salvation,
all so you may believe
nirvana is possible;

i have tortured myself with lies
so, you have belief in a better life.

the only truth i know
is
i would crucify myself
if i knew
it would bring me more comfort
than it would bring you
sorrow.

SCARS GROWN IN A GARDEN

when i wake up in the hotel-bathtub after an overdose
i stare out the small square bathroom window
and see streetlights illuminate through the morning fog.
their hues like translucent new copper pennies.

as my memory is in fog too,
i remember when you didn't mean to say
    "i think you're stealing my heart."
on that halloween eve   all those years ago,

    i abuse who you remember me as
    so, i can forget
    the person you once knew.

i hate every constellation now,

every number eleven
every day in november
every birthday present i have ever given,
because
they all remind me of you.

after i read the letter you sent me
that said

> *"i've always been in love with you,*
> *i am just*
> *ashamed of how i feel."*

i swam naked in the pacific ocean
high on psilocybin.

the waves   began to flow through my body,
like water through clenched palms,
and i prayed
they would wash me clean
of everything you didn't want.

       and i think about the time
i finally kissed you without your permission.
giving you everything i ever wanted
before the first time
i said goodbye to you.

as a child
i was terrified to grow up alone, though
being with you
gave me the confidence
of a hundred immortal men.

and remember the first time
you ever held my hand.
your hair was blonde then,

but now your hair is brown.
now you grow your own vegetables, green tomatoes.
and live happily with your parents
who at a time i felt like i was an only son to.
and still,

you have that gray and black ganesh tattoo
on your right shoulder
i sat beside you for nine hours to receive.

since we first met
your beauty has expanded,
       you are what the universe aspires to become.

it was on august 28th, remember?
when you walk into our college freshman class,
and that teacher of ours,
somehow by fate,
paired us to work together,
all while she didn't know
i would soon shoot heroin
to forget you.

and now,
somehow,
with over 8 years sober
i still
       hate every constellation,

hate every number eleven

hate every day in november

and hate every birthday present   i have ever given,

but   for some reason
i
still

       cannot hate you.

RUSTED UGLY

sometimes like now
i wrap my arms
around my body
just to remember
what it feels like to be cared for

as when i was that time
i haven't told anyone of:

>a single 7-year-old girl sings
>'Hallelujah'
>as a choir of angels
>on the street corner
>
>a woman, a stranger,
>finds me listening
>lent up against a brick wall.
>her arms wrap around my torso
>and the unfallen tears in my eyes
>fall.

now,
i talk with children to feel more confident.
i think they believe i am a god to them.

last night i talked with my neighbor,

he told me his mother just died
while
he sat beside her
at her hospital bed,

all i asked him for was a cigarette
and he gave me more than i wanted to receive.

he saw me standing with my parents the next morning,
i was too full of guilt to make an introduction,
my mother and father just stood there silent.

now, i stand silent while i watch birds.
they dance their dance through the air together
without a single touch
onto the other;
nature reminds me how to be playful.

while i stand here, again, i remember
        i was made *too mechanical.*

UNHEARD PRAYER

i am drunk. passed out
beside the toilet
in the upstairs bathroom
of my parent's house.

i harm myself to be accepted
by people
who i will never meet again.

this memory of when
i ran away from home,
since
my feelings of
i cannot escape this skin
came again.

when you tell me
what your opinions of me are
with your lack of understanding,
makes me become
that insecure 4-year-old boy
once more.

right now,
it is three in the morning
and mom cannot sleep
since i have not returned home.

i pray
mom and i
will one day
have more to speak of
than just
each other's traumas
before one of us die.

CEMETERIES EVERYWHERE

on the side of the sidewalk
there is a blizzard of flies
communed above the corpse of a baby bird,
i've arrived at a funeral.

smoking a cigarette,
self-mutilation –

masochism
bondage and discipline
dominance-submission,

there is
a great lust for escape,
and
there is no way out.

     "when i was 9
     dad died. then
     6 months later
     my little brother died, then
     it was just my mom and i
     from there on."
     she told me at her birthday party.

i don't talk to people anymore,
i feel discomfort enough without them.

flick this cigarette butt, watch the ember descend
      – explode
burst upon the pavement.

and i walk away knowing
i cannot have stop god's plan from occurring;

it is too beautiful outside to believe
pain exists   and yet still   i hear
another buzz
begin.

      it is 73 degrees –
the sun permeates through
the petals of this young red rose
and they become translucent
like my skin does under a flash of light,

it has veins
just as i do.

ABSENT HEART

in the dinner room
you call me
"kid"
and in my body
i am *grotesque*
all over again,

you people
who think i'm their friend;
who i'll never let know
the man i really am
behind this tarnished skin.

i pretend
i loved my teenage self
that no longer exists in the mirror.

i watched tears
form in my eyes
for years and years
and now
they are frozen.

a hypothermia
my heart has
from your absent touch.

i'm too afraid of rejection
to strive for your acceptance,
i am a better man alone.

i leave.

i leave before
i ever give you a chance
to be welcomed in,
into my arms,
just as all the others
have never been,

i am happier without a home.

A LOUD FLEETING FLAME

having sex with a 44-year-old mother,
remember her long white   purple hair
and perfect   pale fake breasts.
    i can only climax
      as she says,
          "i'm your step-sister!".
god do i miss her.

i wore her lingerie
while out to lunch.
i wish i still had that
white lace-thong of hers.

when i touch her face for the last time
i hold her hand and speak this truth:
    i cannot be the father
    to a child that isn't mine.

i awoke in my new bed that no one has laid with me in yet,
unlike the last that held all the stains that meant everything to me,
as if we tattooed our madness into its cotton;
    please, come be who ruins this newfound virginity.

i am naked again.
i stand in front of this open apartment-window
while i stare down upon the street
       i am much older than a child now,
          i didn't want to become the man i am.

the moon begins to be consumed
by the lights of this awaking city,
dissolving into the sky
like a favorite memory
of mine.

IMMORTAL STAINS

someone new lives in the house i grew up in,
a stranger is asleep where i'd shoot heroin,
i want to mail a letter to there
that reveals everything,
      "my blood is still on the bedroom ceiling?".

when father broke his wrist,
fell off the scooter, remember?
after he sped down the hill   shoeless
and crashed
after he tried to teach his children
what to have fun is.
wrapped his exposed bone   in a paper towel
before he drove himself to the hospital;
      i'm embarrassed of my childhood.

today, i pray for the capacity to love someone.
my shoulders are pulled back and this chin is held high,
      and i lie to myself that i am able;

in times of doubt,
agnosticism has prevented me
      from jumping off
          this apartment's balcony.

it is 1:41 a.m.
and soon another day
in which
i reject
the name i was given
will begin.

    i have multiple mental illnesses,
    and don't know the dosage
    of medication
    for making my own happiness;

i feel i am about to have a heart attack.
will weeks pass until someone finally finds my rotted body?
finds me wearing nothing
and smiling.

how do i sell my soul
to the god i should have believed in?
i want to see the face
of who finds me.

a stranger's eyes
are always so beautiful
when my naked body
is reflected in them.

EMPTINESS IS EVIL

i'm here at the airport to pick you up.
you've been in opiate withdrawals for 2 days
and still i find a way
        to soon fall in love with you;
with your black hair cut short
as you said your mother's was when she was alive;

i worry about you,
        know i will
until you and her are together
just as you wish you two were.

when i realize
"to love"
is to do no harm
you have already run
from under my arms.

broken became our unbreakable bond
as i failed again to rectify the damage i had done.
you gave me far too many tries
just as any other angel would;
i feel i have been a satan of a man.

i still don't know how to apologize
for the pain i didn't intend to cause you:
        is my love just a malicious weapon?

i should have said
"i love you"
when i felt
your warm toes up against my shin
and thigh
but now i lie to myself
about never knowing
how *security* feels.

you   and i
and no one else
could ever write
the poetry
we did to each other
since we knew
it was all that bound us together,
       "give me those scared wrists to kiss
       so, they will be healed by these timid lips."

i miss your hips.

i miss our silence,

i miss not knowing
what
the absence of
you
is.

GOTHIC BODY

from the eastside of the country
the sun slits across the sky's stomach
      cesarean sections
the blood of hot-white bleach
leaks across a black canvas

     beneath those
cut open skies
       an ocean of slumber awakens
and birds in great numbers   blacken the moon

my conception happens
birthed at 11:59 at night.

one hand holds the moments around our family table
that time of when –   (these five fingers recoil into a fist)
    this body doesn't allow a remembrance.

we pray to invisible beings to save us,
tattoo of crucified-jesus in black ink upon my thigh.
i try to make you believe i am a good enough person,
     for years i've been insecure about my lying skin.

my face has become a cemetery
for sins i've committed.
i reminisce
and remember all the apologies
i have never given.

    i've been so close to death
    so many times
    i deserve to know
    what to die is like.

my grandfather's funeral is an open casket.
there isn't enough makeup upon his face
to cover the scars he placed upon his children;

    my siblings and i
    won't have children
    and
    our family-tree
    will finally die.

ETERNAL WITHDRAWAL

you didn't know me yet when i'd get high.
in my mother's car, recline the driver's seat back,
wrap the seat belt around my left bicep
use the needle again   and –

(self-abuse was the only talent i had then.)

before you knew me
i would watch pornography
of women who look just like you.
as if i was practicing
how to not touch you
while i was in love   and you were
in a distant country.

i saw one of those fold-up bicycles, like the one you let me ride
      and took away with you when you moved away,
          the same shade of seafoam aqua blue,
it reminded me
i will still cry over my cherished memories of you.

those clouds, remember? that flow over the mountainous hills
of the city where we spent new years day   and night together,
      where we were the most in love with each other,
        i don't tell anyone of how much i hate that city.

i do want to share my bed with someone new.
someone i can grow old with,
share my floral sheets
with somebody i love
and trust, though, now,
      flowers
only remind me
death exists.

THE GREAT VACATION

in the mirror i stand
with this suicide in my mind,

a fire that burns happiness
down to a lavender ash

behind this face, jaded and aged,
decrepit
as a once hopeful boy's is

      i remember the illusion of our love
fade
like
that happiness you so often spoke of.

remember those dozen sunflowers,
unable to stop
the bleeding
of your *deep* prepubescent wounds?
    they reminded me
    i am incapable too
    of making healing happen for you.
    —

i hear a pound in my head that yells
    but i loved you
even when your body wasn't around.

    we'll be together again soon
is my beautiful delusion.
it keeps me safe
while i lay in this frigid bed.
    –

our eyes no longer intertwine
so, in my mind
a beautiful demonic torment blooms.
    –

    and as i awake again
drenched in a cold sweat
i remember
the hatred i have
for this name of mine, then

the questions and devils come.
making their case *over and over*
that i will be happier dead.

while i lay here alone
i imagine
the sky on fire,
amber sky
      over the ocean
amethyst roaring waves
reflecting back orange and purple.

there
i no longer hear
the deafening presence
of being so alone,

my laughter
dances with the waves
as they crash.

FLOWERS AREN'T ALWAYS BEAUTIFUL

it is 8:27 in the morning
my sister just misses the school bus
while i am 19 years old
and addicted to oxycontin pills.

she asks me for a ride
so, she can arrive on time at 9, but
i am in withdrawals   and
need to drive to my drug dealer's house
across town
before
he leaves with what i need,
i abandon my sister again.

my sister lives twenty-five hundred miles away from me now.
her and i see each other
at most
three times a year,
    i don't know why i can only
    love those dearest to me
    from a far.

it is 4:31 p.m.
on a tuesday   and
i haven't spoken a word yet
to anyone,

i am on a run through the city.
my shirt is off
and
my back reddens from the sun;

everywhere i go, there i am.

it is christmas day in 4 days,
december 21st   at 12:21,

i see angels in numbers
and they see me
in my darkest hour.

one night back in late september
everything turned black
and it was beautiful.
so beautiful i begun to believe
in a better future
so much so,
i released my grip
on that strap of brown leather
that i had wrapped
around my neck.

it's christmas morning and
my sister
gifts me a book of poetry
and i gift her
a candle
shaped as a teepee,

we say to the other
i'll see you soon
and
i love you.

it is december 29th today,
    and still
my sister and i
only know each other
as well as we always have;

    i pray
    family reunions
    never happen
    because of funerals.

GREEN MEMORY

i write this poem on the back of a love letter,
a love letter wrote to whom i thought
was my lost soulmate,
a love letter
i never sent.

her and i haven't spoken
since
she chose to cause our separation.
i remember her last name still.

not the name, but
its origin.
she was adopted.

>a neighbor becomes
>a perfect mother
>who teaches
>a teenage girl
>about
>unconditional love   and
>unconventional   families,
>and how
>they harmonize
>so perfect together,

the rain   and sun
in the spring-   summer day.

today
i smelled
fresh cut grass
in the middle of
our
big city,

        and there was wind
        that was young.

UNANSWERED PAIN

i roll down a grass hill
i am a seven-year-old
i am a child as a child is supposed to be,
i itch my hair and find blood on my hand,
i don't know i've hit my head on a metal rail.
the doctor treats me like his own
and lets me keep his staple gun,
        pain and love are inseparable.

in middle school i am the awkward and ugly teacher's son.
the only way i know how to make friends
is to freely give candy to my classmates,
why
aren't i enough on my own?

since then, i have learned how to hold conversation
and have grown into my body
        and my mother is retired now.
for years my hands have not needed to distribute anything, but
my saturday nights are still eventless
and still i feel lost   and
don't know why i can't find anyone to love me.
i feel i've been a twelve-year-old
for seventeen years,
am i at fault somehow?

in this apartment i rent,
in this
103 degrees apartment
i cannot afford,
the underwear i wear is red.
my face is red.
my anger is red,
i am the bull
and the matador
again tonight.

    11:49

    my time to romance with suicide:
    "the great vacation" i've named it.

i sit in the shower
as sharp cold-water streams down my back,
i shiver a sound and become a deranged drum.
    i become numb.
    and become one with the pain
    like
the flower
drowning in rain.

TEMPERATURE OF WHITE

on the front porch

before the sun has risen
whistling with the birds

as they awaken
i've been awake all night

we are an orchestra
no one else is around, not the neighbors
      not the parents.

each time
they whistle back to me
i feel
i am understood
for the first time.

they make the sound
of the name i was given
before i was born.

       they knew
       the color of my eyes

       before ever open.

when i go to sleep
i think and know
they are always
there

for me.

       today,
       a single divine dove
       is tattooed
       upon my neck.

RED AS GOD

while i hug you goodbye on the side of the street
my ring-finger caress the ridge of your rib
and i thank the universe
for all the times
i defied death
before this moment now.

    i fall asleep drunk behind the wheel of my father's station wagon,
    it is 3 in the morning,
    while i parallel park in front of his house,
    i recall a patrol car is parked and watching.
    there is a gram of white-china heroin in my sock.
    i wake up in my bed the next day.

now, i am alone in this apartment studio.
in the bed we slept together for weeks in
and lived in our fantasy
that had been born from our loneliness,

with a dragon's head
tattooed on your back in black ink
and a stallion galloping through water
on mine just the same
i remember the time we met by mistake
and began to believe that tripled numbers are meaningful,

        you leave my house today at 4:44 in the afternoon –

now, i am alone in the studio.

this place you cared for me in
when i had that violent sickness,

        for three days i sweat profusely
        and can't leave the bathroom,
        i drift out and in of consciousness,

        blissfully welcomed back to life
        by your back lit silhouette.

during then
i had this hallucination,

        on the edge
        of a pale white beach
        you dance unclothed
        with your long blond hair.
        unifying with empty space
        and sand,
        while the black sky
        is cracked open by lightning
        and
        you mouth words to me
        i cannot hear.

BAPTIZED BY PAIN

i lay on this apartment's amber wood floorboards,
the ceiling fan clicks, it is a diseased heart,

i feel i am made of cement. stiff and gray, covered in
        the wretched flesh
        i have been so afraid of.   anyone,
        please come be my savior,

        come
        pour
        your sins into my ear,
        break me free
        with the utterance of your fears.

i pray my parents die in their sleep.
take them away in silent peace
without having to say goodbye to me,

without having to be embarrassed by
the person i have caused myself to become.

and i curse you god,
you and your son
who have caused my confusion
of whom and what i should believe in,
i am a good man
without having you save me of my sins.

there is a taste of copper in my mouth again,
i need the soap   force fed to me
used to cleanse
the verbal demons out.

i wish our parents had hurt us,
i could justify why
i am this fragile.
but you two
are   so successful
and i am just
their other   middle child.

behind this apartment's manilla walls
i hear chirps of a dying bird
and remember
i've been dying here
for quite some time too,

i am not the only one
imprisoned how i am.

in through the window
a beam of quartz sunlight
streams from that sun
i have forgotten of,

the door out of here
unlocks from the inside, and i
stretch these tattooed arms out
like the wings
of a disfigured   baby dove
who has finally
        decided to fly.

BORN FROM COFFINS

(i)

yesterday morning while i drive to work i cry.
i remember this isn't the first time i have   and
i think to myself,
> drive to the gun range already   and
> hold the steel in your hand,
> learn what it feels like
> when a dream finally becomes real.

i remember
when you told me how
she
had shot herself
and how
you found her on the living room floor
while
her kitchen sink faucet
still ran
in the background,

i envy such swiftness of decision.

as i think her name
my heart arrythmias
from an inspiration.

(ii)

we are across the table from each other.
inexpensive soup is shared between us
and you tell me
you don't perform oral sex
because you're afraid
of esophagus cancer,

i thought
love
is about sacrifice,
right?

like how i sacrificed my happiness for you
and still
you never told me
you're attracted to this face i have.

since then, you've shown me
the lies behind your porcelain skin.
i can now see
the trauma
unfulfilled dreams afflict.
thank you,

i will never dream of you again.

(iii)

my eyes are shut.
in the bathroom
while all the lights are off
while no one is home,
i whisper into the mirror

    "you're so afraid
    of being alone."

i believe
i would have been better off an orphan   but
beliefs
are just beliefs,
and i see i have another missed call
from my father,

i have been the thief
of so many people's happiness,

i take a deep breath
and don't move.

(iv)

i hear you laugh about me.

and i feel sorry for you
as you believe
god made you
just as you are. and i remember
the child i once was
before i learned
self-inflicted harm can heal unwanted wounds.

remember,
today is the anniversary
of the day
i decided
to let you shoot me up with heroin.

it's the choices i've made
that have always been
what aided in
my own destruction,

suicide isn't the cure, but,
it is an end.

(v)

i walk outside.
stick my toes into the grass.
into the dirt, into the ground.

i begin to dig
and as i do
soil builds underneath my fingernails,

as i become
more and more
fully beneath this ground,

a serenity comes.

i pack the cold black earth
up against my eyes,
from me a smile grows.

dirt fills in the gaps of my teeth
and my ears
and
it all becomes so quiet,
exquisite,
> *my whole life is still in front of me,*
> *and i am a child*
> *once again.*

Suicide takes the life from almost 50,000 Americans every year.
Today is December 3rd, 2023, and I do not plan be one of them this year.

Suicide feels like the only option when suicidal thoughts come, though it isn't the only decision you can choose to make.

Poetry, therapy, fitness, and community have helped me get through my thoughts of suicide.
There are ways out.

I don't know what next year has in store for me, but
I know I will do whatever I have to do so I stay off next year's suicide list too.

Email me at Flowersarentalwaysbeautiful@gmail.com ,
I'm here for you if you feel like no one else is.

www.ingramcontent.com/pod-product-compliance
Lightning Source LLC
Chambersburg PA
CBHW022119090426
42743CB00008B/927